Biff and Chip went to stay with Gran.
They went to stay for a week.
"Be good," called Mum.
"Don't worry," said Gran. "I will."

Gran's house was small. It had two
bedrooms. Biff and Chip had to sleep in
the same bedroom.

Biff wanted the bed by the door. Chip
wanted the bed by the window.
"That's good," said Gran.

Gran took Biff and Chip for a walk.
They went to the woods. Biff saw some
blackberries. She wanted to pick some.

Gran had some plastic bags. She gave
one to Biff and Chip.

"We can make some blackberry jam,"
she said.

Gran made the blackberry jam. Biff and
Chip helped. Chip made some labels and
Biff licked the spoon.

They made nine jars of jam.
"You can take a jar home for Kipper,"
said Gran. "And a jar for Wilf and Wilma."

The children loved Gran's house. It was very old. It had a big fireplace. Biff helped Gran light the fire.

Chip helped Gran get some logs.
"Do you have ghosts?" he asked.
Gran laughed.
"There are no such things," she said.

They sat by the fire. Gran made some
toast. Biff wanted to try the new jam.
"It's still too hot," said Gran.

Chip had a new game. It was called
Haunted House.

"Can we play Haunted House, before
we go to bed?" he asked.

It was time for bed. Gran got Chip a hot
water bottle.

"*Is* this house haunted?" asked Biff.

"Don't worry," laughed Gran. "I don't
have ghosts in my house. There are no
such things."

Biff and Chip couldn't sleep. Biff had an idea. She wanted to play a joke on Chip. She had a torch in the bed.

Biff put the sheet over her head. She
switched on the torch. The sheet glowed.
"Whooooooo! I am a ghost," said Biff.

Chip laughed. He wasn't frightened. He
pulled the sheet off Biff.

"That was a good joke," he said.

Biff and Chip heard a noise. It came from outside.

"Whoooo! Whoooo!" went the noise.

"Oh no!" said Biff. "It's a ghost."

Chip looked out of the window.

"It's not a ghost!" he laughed. "It's an owl. Come and look."

Biff and Chip looked outside.
"Oh no!" said Chip. "I can see a ghost.
It *is* a ghost this time."

Biff and Chip ran to Gran's room.

"Gran! Gran!" called Biff. "There's a ghost outside."

But Gran wasn't in bed.

Biff and Chip ran downstairs.

"Gran!" called Biff. "Where are you?
We've seen a ghost."
But Gran wasn't downstairs.

The door opened. Biff and Chip were
frightened.

"Oh no!" they said.

Gran came in.

"We were frightened," said Chip. "You
looked like a ghost."
Gran laughed.
"I'm not a ghost," she said.

"I don't have ghosts," said Gran. "But I
do have two little monsters!"
Gran laughed and so did Biff and Chip.